Author: B. Mater Cofield   Illustrator: Aila Naveed

All rights to this literary work, "I Am Everything And Everything is Me," including but not limited to text, illustrations, and any associated materials, are hereby reserved. No part of this book may be reproduced, distributed, or transmitted in any form or by any means, including photocopying, recording, or other electronic or mechanical methods, without the prior written permission of the author, except for brief quotations embodied in critical reviews and certain other noncommercial uses permitted by copyright law.

I am the brilliant, blue sky.

I am the shining bright light of the moon.

I am the healing warmth of the sun.

I am the freedom of the north star.

I am the celestial planet in the galaxy.

I am the ripples of the ocean.

I am a long narrow blade of grass.

I am the floral fragrance in flowers.

I am the tall, enchanting trees in the forest.

I am a mystic, majestic mountain.

I am the sweet kiss of the rain.

I am the beautiful, vibrant colors of the rainbow.

I am the fresh air that I breathe.

I am the sweet melody of the hummingbird.

I am the cool, moist soil beneath my feet.

I Am Everything And Everything Is Me.
We are One Song.

www.ingramcontent.com/pod-product-compliance
Lightning Source LLC
Chambersburg PA
CBHW041815040426
42451CB00001B/5